HER MAJESTY
QUEEN
ELIZABETH II

TO COMMEMORATE THE DIAMOND JUBILEE
OF HER MAJESTY QUEEN ELIZABETH II

HER MAJESTY QUEEN ELIZABETH II

DIAMOND JUBILEE SOUVENIR

ANNIE BULLEN

Front cover: A radiant young queen: Her Majesty Queen Elizabeth II.

Back cover: Her Majesty Queen Elizabeth II and the Duke of Edinburgh, photographed in 2007, the year of their Diamond Wedding anniversary.

Title pages: Her Majesty Queen Elizabeth II and Prince Philip on her coronation day, 2 June 1953.
The Queen visits the University of Cambridge, April 2011.

Frontispiece: Princess Elizabeth in the State Apartments at Buckingham Palace, 1946.

Opposite: The official coronation crown: St Edward's Crown was made in 1661 for the coronation of Charles II and is based on the original crown worn by Edward the Confessor in 1065.

Publication in this form copyright © Pitkin Publishing 2011.
Text copyright © Pitkin Publishing 2011.

Written by Annie Bullen.
The moral right of the author has been asserted.

Editorial consultant: Brian Hoey. The publisher would like to thank Brian Hoey for his editorial guidance.

Edited by Gill Knappett.
Picture research by Jan Kean.
Cover designed by Katie Beard.
Designed by Glad Stockdale.
Production by Karen Kinnear.

A CIP catalogue for this book is available from the British Library.
Published by Pitkin Publishing, Healey House, Dene Road, Andover, Hampshire, SP10 2AA, UK.
www.pitkin-guides.com

Printed in Great Britain.
ISBN 978-1-84165-373-0   1/11

CONTENTS

HAPPY & *Glorious*

Three queens of Great Britain, silent and watchful, each veiled and dressed in mourning, stood closely together in the shadows of Westminster Hall as subdued crowds filed quietly past the bier of the man who had been their king. His mother, his wife and his daughter were there, like his people, to pay homage to King George VI who had neither expected nor wanted the Crown, but who had carried out the duty thrust upon him in exemplary fashion. Now his daughter, the young Queen Elizabeth II, would do the same.

On 6 February 2012, Her Majesty Queen Elizabeth II will have been Sovereign for 60 years, and the nation will rejoice as she celebrates her Diamond Jubilee. And indeed it will be a cause for celebration as she has made it a happy and glorious reign for her subjects, despite the unremitting hard work of the daily responsibilities faced by the monarchy.

She was just 25 years old, the mother of two young children and happily married to the Duke of Edinburgh, when her father, King George VI, died. Although she and Philip must have hoped that they would be able to experience a relatively uncomplicated life as a young married couple for longer than the five years they had already enjoyed,

Elizabeth, who since the age of 10 had known that her destiny was to become Queen, never demurred. 'My heart is too full for me to say more to you today than I shall always work as my father did,' she told her Privy Counsellors at St James's Palace as she made the accession declaration before them on 8 February 1952.

From that day – more than half a century ago – she has been as good as her word. She acceded to the throne when Britain was still struggling out of post-war financial stringencies. It soon became clear that the monarchy, although still a beloved

Left: Three queens in mourning. On 11 February 1952, the new Queen Elizabeth, her grandmother, Queen Mary, and her mother, Queen Elizabeth the Queen Mother, stand silently at Westminster Hall in tribute to King George VI, who had just died.

Right: The 10-year-old Princess Elizabeth and her father, the Duke of York, in the grounds of their London home, 145 Piccadilly, in July 1936 – the year in which events unfolded which meant she would one day be Queen.

institution, would have to change with the times, becoming more accessible and informal. The changes started gradually. In the early years of her reign she supported the introduction of life peerages for both men and women – meaning that those without hereditary titles could sit and vote in the House of Lords. In 1957 the long-established and exclusive presentation of 'debutantes' at Buckingham Palace was replaced by more informal garden parties and luncheons for people from all walks of life. Not long afterwards the public was able to visit the former chapel at Buckingham Palace, now The Queen's Gallery, to see exhibitions chosen from the royal art collection.

Queen Elizabeth has presided over these changes gracefully, accepting her role as a constitutional monarch whose duties as Head of State are skilfully balanced with a very human touch.

Left: The Queen, standing in a Land Rover, is cheered by a large gathering of ex-servicemen and women at Parliament House, Canberra, during the royal tour of Australia in early 1954.

Right: Two young Aboriginal girls are introduced to The Queen and Prince Philip in Townsville, Queensland, during the 1954 royal tour of Australia.

Far right: The Queen, in a formal evening gown, is accompanied by Australian Prime Minister Robert Menzies as she meets guests at a State Ball in Canberra in 1954.

Below right: Prince Edward, The Queen's youngest son, was still a baby when the family gathered at Windsor for this photograph in early 1965. Princess Anne stands by her mother while Charles, Prince of Wales is on his father's right. Young Prince Andrew holds onto the pram.

Becoming Queen of the United Kingdom involved more than getting to know the people of Great Britain. In the months and years following her coronation, Her Majesty – accompanied as always by the Duke of Edinburgh, who received the title 'Prince of the United Kingdom' in 1957 – travelled not only the length and breadth of the British Isles, but also embarked on tours of the Commonwealth. She became the first reigning monarch to visit Australia and New Zealand and was received in 1954 with enthusiasm by people to whom the British monarchy must have previously seemed remote.

Despite the demanding duties of an often gruelling daily programme concerned with affairs of state, and fulfilling an unending round of engagements both at home and abroad, Her Majesty has balanced these with family life and her love of country pursuits, such as walking, riding and fishing. Perhaps Elizabeth and Philip's duties and travelling in those early years of her reign delayed the growth of their family, for their firstborn, Prince Charles, was already 11 and their daughter, Princess Anne, nine when Prince Andrew was born in 1960, followed four years later by Prince Edward.

The role of the monarchy may have developed and changed over the years but it is consistent in standing as a symbol outside party politics, representing a focus for the loyalty of the nation, while still embodying the sense of history that is so much part of the British way of life. Her Majesty is also a focal point for the members of the Commonwealth who are bound together by common ideals and interests. There continues to be a respect for honesty and virtue, and The Queen displays these qualities – alongside a quiet sense of humour, shared with her husband who has been a constant, her 'rock'.

Only her great-great-grandmother, Queen Victoria, has reigned longer. As Queen Elizabeth II celebrates her 60 years on the throne, she does so in the knowledge that she is presiding over a modern monarchy that has moved with the times, without sacrificing the glorious tradition and pageantry that is renowned and admired the world over.

ROYAL *Milestones*

1926 Princess Elizabeth Alexandra Mary is born in London on 21 April to the Duke and Duchess of York; she is third in line of succession to the throne

1930 Princess Margaret Rose, Princess Elizabeth's sister, is born on 21 August

1936 King Edward VIII abdicates. Princess Elizabeth's father becomes King George VI (and the last Emperor of India, until 1948). The Princess is now 'heiress presumptive'

1937 The new Royal Family move into Buckingham Palace

1939 Princess Elizabeth meets Prince Philip for the first time, at Dartmouth

1940 The Princesses Elizabeth and Margaret are evacuated to Windsor Castle; Elizabeth makes a wartime radio broadcast to the children of the Empire

1945 The Princesses Elizabeth and Margaret mingle with the crowds celebrating the end of the war

1946 Princess Elizabeth and Prince Philip become engaged

1947 Princess Elizabeth and her sister tour South Africa with their parents; Elizabeth and Philip are married on 20 November in Westminster Abbey

1948 Prince Charles is born on 14 November

1950 Princess Anne is born on 15 August

1951 Princess Elizabeth and the Duke of Edinburgh undertake a tour of Canada and the USA

1952 Princess Elizabeth's father, King George VI, dies on 6 February; the new Queen flies home from East Africa

1953 The Queen is crowned on 2 June in Westminster Abbey

1954 The Queen and the Duke of Edinburgh tour Australia and New Zealand; the Royal Yacht *Britannia* is commissioned

1957 The royal couple visit the USA; the first televised Queen's Christmas message is broadcast from Sandringham

1960 The Queen changes the family name to Mountbatten-Windsor; Prince Andrew is born on 19 February

1963	The Queen visits Australia, the trip coinciding with Canberra's Jubilee celebrations
1964	Prince Edward is born on 10 March
1967	Royal visit to Canada for centenary celebrations
1969	Prince Charles is invested Prince of Wales at Caernarfon Castle
1972	Silver wedding celebrations for The Queen and the Duke of Edinburgh; their first grandchild, Peter Philips, is born
1977	The Queen celebrates her Silver Jubilee
1981	The Queen's son and heir, Prince Charles, marries Lady Diana Spencer
1982	Pope John Paul II becomes the first Pope to visit Britain for 450 years; Prince William, third in line to the throne, is born
1986	The Queen becomes the first British monarch to visit China
1987	Princess Anne receives the title 'Princess Royal'
1991	The Queen is the first British Head of State to address a joint meeting of the US Congress
1992	The Queen meets Nelson Mandela in Zimbabwe; a fire causes severe damage at Windsor Castle
1997	Diana, Princess of Wales dies in Paris; The Queen and the Duke of Edinburgh mark 50 years of marriage
1999	The Queen attends openings of the Welsh Assembly and the new Scottish Parliament
2000	Celebrations for the Queen Mother's 100th birthday
2002	Both the Queen Mother and Princess Margaret die in the year of The Queen's Golden Jubilee
2005	The Prince of Wales and Mrs Camilla Parker Bowles marry in Windsor; Camilla takes the title 'Duchess of Cornwall'
2011	The Queen's grandson, Prince William, marries Catherine Middleton at Westminster Abbey, and they become the Duke and Duchess of Cambridge; The Queen and the Duke of Edinburgh celebrate 65 years of marriage
2012	Her Majesty celebrates her Diamond Jubilee

Lilibet THE EARLY YEARS

W hen Elizabeth Alexandra Mary, first granddaughter of King George V, was born on 21 April 1926, there was general rejoicing – but little speculation or expectation that one day this latest addition to the Royal Family would become queen. Her father, Prince Albert ('Bertie'), was the King's younger son. His elder brother, the new baby's 'Uncle David', Prince of Wales, was not married, but there was no reason to suppose that he would not take a wife, produce an heir and succeed his father to the British throne.

The little Elizabeth was brought up very much as any upper-class child of the time and doted on by both sets of grandparents. She was fortunate that her mother, the former Lady Elizabeth Bowes-Lyon, born in 1900, was the second youngest of the Earl of Strathmore's ten children, raised by generous and understanding parents in rural Hertfordshire and the medieval Glamis Castle in Scotland where she enjoyed a close-knit, energetic and loving

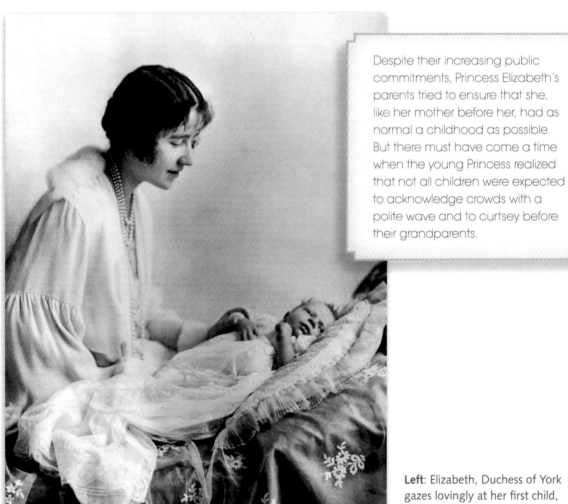

Despite their increasing public commitments, Princess Elizabeth's parents tried to ensure that she, like her mother before her, had as normal a childhood as possible. But there must have come a time when the young Princess realized that not all children were expected to acknowledge crowds with a polite wave and to curtsey before their grandparents.

Left: Elizabeth, Duchess of York gazes lovingly at her first child, Elizabeth, future Queen of England.

Right: Nanny Clara Knight ('Alla') with her young charge, Princess Elizabeth, in 1927.

family life. Baby Elizabeth's father, the Duke of York, who courted Lady Elizabeth assiduously for two years before she agreed to marriage, was of a different temperament altogether. His lack of self-confidence, worsened by a persistent stammer, made his a diffident and shy nature. But marriage, the birth of his first child – and eventually the services of a good speech therapist – helped the introverted Bertie gain a measure of confidence that was to stand him in good stead when later events took an unexpected turn.

When Elizabeth was almost a year old her parents embarked, without her, on a six-month tour of Australia. Her father, bolstered by lessons from his therapist, Lionel Logue, was able to deliver speeches more easily, while her mother, although sad at leaving her young daughter for such a length of time, did so in the knowledge that the grandparents, aided by nanny Clara Knight ('Alla'), would give their daughter all the care and attention she needed. The baby was spoiled by King George, 'Grandpa England' (who had been a severe and exacting father to his own sons), and spent time with her Strathmore grandparents as well.

Once the Duke and Duchess of York arrived home (with three tons of gifts and several parrots from Australian well-wishers for their baby) the family settled into 145 Piccadilly, just across Green Park from Buckingham Palace. The Duchess gave birth to a second daughter, Margaret Rose, in August 1930 at Glamis Castle – the first royal baby born in Scotland for 330 years. And it was a young Princess Margaret who, attempting to talk to her elder sister, uttered the word 'Lilibet', which is still used as an affectionate family name.

As Margaret grew out of babyhood, the two sisters, often isolated from the company of other children, became close, sharing a happy childhood. Princess Elizabeth was taught at home, first by her mother with whom she learnt the alphabet, a little French, drawing, music and dancing. This expanded to include geography and history when Scottish nanny Marion Crawford, known as 'Crawfie', became her governess.

Margaret joined the schoolroom when she was old enough and, despite their parents' public engagements, a balance was struck so that as much time as possible was spent with the children in London and at the Royal Family's country homes.

But life was soon to change – not only for the young Princess and her family, but for the nation as a whole. Across the world countries were going to war. In 1936 the Spanish Civil War started; the following year Japan began to attack China; and in 1938 Hitler occupied Vienna and made moves against Czechoslovakia. Fear of another great war was beginning to spread in Britain, but the unexpected upheaval for the Duke and Duchess of York and their daughters came with the death of Elizabeth's grandfather, King George V, in January 1936.

In 1931 Elizabeth's parents, the Duke and Duchess of York, were granted the then badly dilapidated Royal Lodge in Windsor Great Park. Extensive renovation turned it into a comfortable country home where 'Lilibet' could ride her Shetland pony, Peggy, help in the garden and enjoy the comparative freedom of a country life.

Left: Princess Elizabeth and her younger sister Princess Margaret are accompanied by their nanny Marion Crawford on a visit to the YMCA headquarters in May 1939.

14

If King George had been perceived as a severe father by his own sons, his granddaughters, on whom he had doted, were fond of him and his death was a sad time for Elizabeth. Dashing Uncle David, her father's older brother, was proclaimed King Edward VIII and, once the funeral was over, took up his constitutional duties. But the new monarch, at 41, was a troubled man. It was an open secret in royal circles and high society that he was infatuated with Mrs Wallis Simpson, an American socialite whom he had first met at a house party in 1931. In January 1936 his dream of marrying Mrs Simpson seemed an impossible one: a British monarch could not marry a divorcee.

It was apparent to the King's ministers and his civil servants that he did not cope well with confidential documents that required his signature, nor was his heart in his daily duties. He told Prime Minister Stanley Baldwin in early November that he intended to marry the woman he loved. Wallis Simpson was divorced from her second husband, Ernest, late in 1936 and on the morning of 10 December Edward's abdication notice was witnessed by his three brothers. The following day it was made legal by Parliament.

And so it was that Albert, Duke of York, the happily married family man, was left to shoulder a heavy burden. He would become King George VI and his beloved daughter, the 10-year-old Elizabeth, was named 'heiress presumptive', next in line to the throne.

Above: 'The Little House' (*Y Bwthyn Bach*), a thatched cottage given to the Princesses Elizabeth and Margaret on Elizabeth's sixth birthday by the people of Wales, still stands in the grounds of Royal Lodge, Windsor. Here the Duke and Duchess of York and their two daughters enjoy the picturesque building.

Right: King George VI and his two daughters, the Princesses Elizabeth (right) and Margaret, riding together in Windsor Great Park in April 1939.

A WARTIME
Princess

On 13 October 1940, a teenager addressed the nation's young people on BBC radio's *Children's Hour*. The war in Europe had entered a second year and Princess Elizabeth spoke to her future subjects at home and across the Commonwealth, exhorting them to keep their spirits up. 'We know, every one of us, that in the end all will be well,' she said.

Elizabeth was just 14, but well aware that she was not to lead a normal or carefree life. Since her father had become Sovereign, being crowned on 12 May 1937 – the day that had been set aside for his brother's coronation – she had received training for her future. Her private life was suddenly in the public domain.

From the age of 10 she became well-versed in the constitution, the role of the monarch and her place in Britain's history. Her father, who had wept at the task that lay ahead when told he would be King, had, with the constant support of his wife, made a conscientious and excellent job of it – especially through the long, dark days of the Second World War.

The young Princesses, coached by their grandmother, Queen Mary, were well prepared for their parents' coronation. The widowed Queen saw to it that they both understood the ancient significance of the ritual and the parts played by the orb and sceptres, the ampulla and the swords. Elizabeth and Margaret wore identical long dresses and specially made lightweight coronets. And if they were taken aback by the thunderous cheering from massed crowds thronging the streets as they drove in a carriage with Queen Mary for the ceremony in Westminster Abbey, they certainly did not show it, acknowledging the applause as they had been taught.

Right: May 1937: a formal photograph of the new Royal Family in their coronation robes.

Elizabeth and Margaret stayed at Balmoral during the first weeks of the war, while the King and Queen rushed back to London. On the beautiful Scottish estate the girls spent almost every waking hour outside. Because many of the household staff were involved in the war effort, they were able to enjoy looking after their ponies without the help of grooms, and could ride with comparative freedom wherever they liked – as long as their police bodyguard could keep them in sight.

But in the New Year, 1940, they were brought back to Windsor, where they became proud of their parents' indefatigable encouragement of the men and women fighting for Britain.

Right: Princess Elizabeth (right), helped by her sister, Margaret, makes a wartime broadcast to the children of Britain and the Empire.

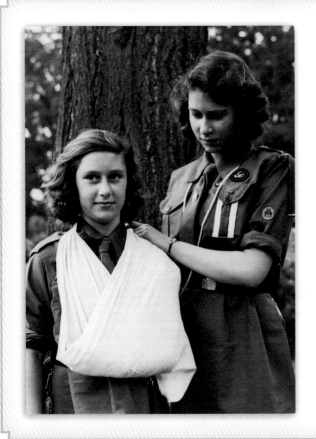

The years between the coronation and the outbreak of war were happy ones for Elizabeth and Margaret who found themselves able to join the Girl Guides and Brownies, based at Buckingham Palace. Their grandmother, Queen Mary, accompanied the girls to galleries and museums, while their governess took them on 'adventures' – a trip to London Zoo or a ride on a tube train. They spent summer holidays in Scotland with their maternal grandmother where they enjoyed family outings in the company of their numerous cousins. The difference in the nature of the girls was already apparent: while Margaret was extrovert and mischievous, her older sister was becoming a thoughtful and considerate young woman.

Left: Princess Elizabeth practises her Girl Guide first aid on her sister in 1942.

Many young people lost part of their childhood to the war and Princess Elizabeth was no exception. Her parents never contemplated sending her and Margaret to the safety of Canada, their mother saying, 'The children won't go without me. I won't leave the King. And the King will never leave.' Instead their war was spent behind the thick walls of Windsor Castle, the cellars bomb-proofed, air-raid shelters outside and the Crown jewels locked away in the vaults.

The sisters could see exactly what was happening. With nanny Alla, they watched as the Battle of Britain lit up the night skies and saw the ghastly red glow of fires in London, little more than 20 miles (32km) away, after a bombing raid.

Following her radio broadcast in 1940, Elizabeth took more responsibility and gleaned a taste of what was to come when she was made Colonel-in-Chief of the Grenadier Guards. She was 15 years old, the youngest person ever to hold such a position. She celebrated her birthday the following year by carrying out her first official engagement – a birthday inspection of the regiment. And so began the round of engagements and duties which she has carried out cheerfully and conscientiously ever since.

Two years later, in 1944, Princess Elizabeth was able to receive official visitors in her private sitting room at Windsor Castle, and appointed her first lady-in-waiting and private secretary, Lady Mary Strachey. Elizabeth became a Counsellor of State, joining her mother the Queen and other members of the Royal Family as an official representative for her father while he was away.

Princess Elizabeth and Prince Philip of Greece and Denmark, as was his full title, were distant cousins, but only came to know each other from 1939, when she was 13 and he an 18-year-old naval cadet at Dartmouth. Elizabeth and her family were travelling on the Royal Yacht *Victoria and Albert* with her 'Uncle Dickie', Lord Louis Mountbatten, who was Philip's real uncle. They called in at Dartmouth where the tall fair-haired cadet, who was to capture her heart, was detailed to look after the two Princesses. Although Elizabeth was too young for romance then, the two were regularly in touch after that meeting.

Above: Princess Elizabeth carries out her first public engagement on her 16th birthday in April 1942 when, as Colonel-in-Chief, she inspects the Grenadier Guards.

Helping the War Effort

But she was determined to play a more active part in the war – albeit for a short time. The young ATS Second Subaltern Her Royal Highness the Princess Elizabeth (serial number 230873) joined up in March 1945, learning how to drive and service heavy lorries and achieving an excellent pass in marksmanship – she had had a lot of practise with firearms on the rifle range at Buckingham Palace. The war in Europe ended just three weeks after she completed her training, so there was little active service, although she maintained many years later that she could change a carburettor on a five-ton truck if necessary.

Right: Princess Elizabeth, training as an ATS mechanic, explains the finer points of a car engine to her mother in 1945.

Below: The war is officially over and a nation celebrates Victory in Europe. Here crowds are gathered outside Buckingham Palace, where the Royal Family appears on the balcony.

On 8 May 1945, Victory in Europe (VE) Day, the two Princesses appeared in the happy line-up on the balcony at Buckingham Palace alongside their parents and Winston Churchill, the Prime Minister. Later they escaped down below, caught up in the cheering, singing and dancing as the crowds celebrated. That was probably the last time that Elizabeth found herself unrecognized, literally just one of the crowd.

A ROYAL *Bride*

Post-war Britain was struggling to come to terms with social and economic changes, but life was bright for Princess Elizabeth, who had fallen in love with Prince Philip. Since their meeting at Dartmouth, where he had passed out as the best cadet and gone on to distinguish himself during the Second World War, he had taken up the Royal Family's invitations to visit, enjoying the company of both sisters and applauding Elizabeth as she appeared as principal boy in the family's Christmas 1943 performance of *Aladdin* at Windsor Castle.

Now the war was over, Elizabeth took on many of her father's engagements, launching ships, attending public functions and taking the salute on military occasions. But she still found time to enjoy dances at Windsor and Sandringham where, despite all the eligible young men lining up to partner her, Philip was the only one the Princess had eyes for. George VI, tired and unwell after the stress of the war, saw what was coming and dreaded losing his beloved daughter.

Left: Wartime entertainment at Windsor Castle included a production of *Aladdin* in which both Princess Elizabeth (left) and Princess Margaret (right) took part.

Wedding gifts came from members of the public from all walks of life, as well as family and friends, and included a hand-knitted cardigan and tea cosy, two pairs of bed socks, salt cellars from the Queen, a bookcase from Queen Mary, and a picnic hamper from Princess Margaret.

A Royal Engagement

When the young couple took matters into their own hands at Balmoral in the last half of 1946 and became engaged to be married, the King agreed – on condition that the engagement remained secret for the time being. It may be that he worried that his elder daughter was merely infatuated, or perhaps he felt that Britain would not accept Philip who – although like Elizabeth is a direct descendent of Queen Victoria – was not a British subject.

But the King need not have feared. His daughter had inherited his own steadfast nature and there would never be another man in her life. The popularity of the Royal Family – who had stayed in London during the war, sharing the dangers and doing all they could to keep morale and spirits lifted – was at an all-time high. The prospect of a royal wedding was just what everyone needed.

In March 1947, while Princess Elizabeth was visiting South Africa, Philip received British citizenship and made it known that he would be called Lieutenant Philip Mountbatten RN. Finally, on 10 July 1947, the engagement was officially announced and Princess Elizabeth wore Philip's ring – a platinum band with diamonds from a tiara once belonging to his mother.

Wedding presents poured in, the wedding date was set for Thursday 20 November and clothing coupons were collected to buy silk for the royal bride's wedding gown. Even Winston Churchill applauded the wedding, calling it, in true Churchillian style, 'A flash of colour on the hard road we travel.'

Above: Princess Elizabeth on her 21st birthday, broadcasting from the gardens of Government House, Cape Town, pledging her service to the people of the British Commonwealth and Empire.

News of the royal engagement was still under wraps in February 1947 when the Royal Family left a snow-bound England to visit South Africa. Princess Elizabeth, separated from Philip for almost three months, celebrated her 21st birthday in Cape Town, making a broadcast which contained a pledge of duty: 'I declare before you all that my whole life, whether it be long or short, shall be devoted to your service ....'

Left: The newly engaged Princess Elizabeth, her engagement ring clearly visible, tucks her arm through that of her fiancé, Lieutenant Philip Mountbatten RN.

Despite early morning rain on that cold November day, the damp streets of London were turned into a glamorous blaze of colour. The Hon. Pamela Mountbatten, one of the eight bridesmaids, called Princess Elizabeth and Prince Philip 'a dream couple': 'He looked tender, she was adoring,' she said.

Out of mothballs came the Household Brigade's colourful ceremonial full-dress uniform, and crowds cheered to see black bearskins with gleaming chinstraps, shining black horses ridden by white-plumed Life Guards carrying drawn swords, and the Royal Horse Guards with their magnificent red-plumed helmets and burnished breastplates. The Foot Guards were equally colourful and splendid, with red-striped trousers and blue tunics.

The bride may have had to save clothing coupons for her gown but it was sumptuous for all that. Dressmaker Norman Hartnell submitted designs for the bridal gown just three months before the wedding, taking inspiration from Botticelli's painting of *Primavera*. His team of 350 seamstresses worked for almost two months on the rich ivory duchesse satin creation, long-sleeved and fitted at the waist, stitching in a spring theme, symbolic in those post-war times, of flowers, leaves and wheat, detailed in thousands of seed pearls, silver thread and tiny sparkling crystals.

The impressive 13-foot (4-m) star-patterned circular train was of embroidered silk tulle. Beneath the gown, the bride slipped her feet into ivory satin high-heeled peep-toed sandals, trimmed with silver and seed-pearl buckles, made by Edward Rayne. Her bouquet was of white orchids, with a sprig of myrtle from a bush grown from the original myrtle in Queen Victoria's wedding bouquet.

Above: Designer Norman Hartnell's sketch of the dress that Princess Elizabeth chose for her wedding.

Inside Westminster Abbey were 2,500 guests, among them six kings and seven queens. The women wore full-length ball gowns and the men morning dress or uniforms. Splendid jewels, necklaces, bracelets and tiaras, which had been locked away during the hostilities, added to the glamour of the occasion.

Thousands had dragged mattresses into The Mall and along the carriage route to Westminster Abbey where they had camped out all night for a glimpse of the royal bride. And there she was, in the great Irish State Coach with her father, King George VI, dressed in his blue and gold uniform of Admiral of the Fleet with its scarlet sash. The young bride was beautiful in her Hartnell gown. Complementing her ensemble was a host of beautiful jewels with family connections. The bride's diamond tiara, belonging to her mother, had been fashioned from an earlier

Above: King George VI takes his daughter, Princess Elizabeth, to join Prince Philip at the altar of Westminster Abbey on her wedding day, 20 November 1947.

Right: The royal couple, now man and wife, walk down the aisle.

tiara made by Collingwood & Co and given to Queen Mary in 1893 by Queen Victoria, as a wedding present. The tiara, re-fashioned for Queen Mary in 1919, was presented to Queen Elizabeth the Queen Mother in 1936. The bride also wore two pearl necklaces – 'Queen Anne' and 'Queen Caroline' – made from 46 and 50 pearls respectively, and always worn together. These were a wedding gift to Elizabeth from her parents. Her dainty pearl and diamond earrings originally belonged to Princess Mary, Duchess of Gloucester. These were bequeathed to her niece, Princess Mary Adelaide, Duchess of Teck in 1857. Subsequently, the Duchess of Teck bequeathed them to her daughter, the future Queen Mary, 40 years later. Queen Mary presented them to her granddaughter, Princess Elizabeth, in January 1947.

The bride and bridegroom returned to Buckingham Palace in the fairy-tale Glass Coach. Just hours before the wedding, Philip, who had renounced his Greek royal title on becoming a British citizen, was created Duke of Edinburgh and was now His Royal Highness.

The royal pair had to appear on the balcony three times to satisfy the calls of a 100,000-strong crowd before they could join their 150 guests in the white and gold supper room for the wedding breakfast, which included dishes named in their honour: *Filet de Sole Mountbatte* and *Bombe Glacée Princesse Elizabet.*

The newly-weds left Buckingham Palace in a shower of rose petals and drove in an open landau through the freezing evening to Waterloo Station. A couple of hot-water bottles were tucked in with them along with Susan, a favourite pet corgi, as they set off to spend the first part of their honeymoon at Broadlands, the Mountbattens' Hampshire home. From there they travelled to Birkhall, a royal hunting lodge on the Balmoral estate in Scotland.

Right: The newly-weds smile and wave to the cheering crowds from the balcony of Buckingham Palace.

The wedding of Princess Elizabeth saw a change in the attitude of the British people towards royalty, an increased feeling of goodwill and pride, and a closeness not often experienced previously. This may have been enhanced by the use for the first time of film cameras and microphones to record the event, so that the the wedding service could be broadcast around the world on BBC radio, and heard in towns and villages, in streets, shops and homes, with televised highlights shown later, including some in cinemas throughout the country.

Left: The first days of the honeymoon were spent at Broadlands, the Romsey home of Earl Mountbatten, uncle of the Duke of Edinburgh.

A Princess
AT HOME & ABROAD

It might seem strange that the newly-weds, who arrived back in London to celebrate the King's birthday on 14 December, had no home of their own but had to 'make do' for a short while with Elizabeth's three-room apartment at Buckingham Palace. The near-derelict Clarence House was being renovated for them and the young couple, needing privacy until the repairs were complete, moved from the Palace, staying in a loaned house in London and then at a rented property near Windsor.

Philip was working at the Admiralty, with time off to support his wife as she undertook engagements and to carry out a few of his own – a gradual start to the efficient and dedicated partnership that they have built over the years. In May 1948, the couple made their first official overseas visit, to France where they experienced the sort of welcome – from rapturous, cheering crowds and intense media attention – that left them in no doubt that their lives would always be lived in the public spotlight.

The visit was a success. The weather was hot, but if Elizabeth, who was expecting their first child, felt the strain, she did not show it. Philip, not used to this level of media intrusion, found it harder to cope. Life became increasingly busy as the public demand on the young couple increased.

Clarence House, next to St James's Palace in London, had been the home of Queen Victoria's son, the Duke of Connaught. On his death in 1942, the dilapidated house, with his late wife's favourite sitting room preserved exactly as she had left it almost 30 years earlier, was used for a while as offices. The necessary repairs for Elizabeth and Philip cost £78,000 (around £2.3 million in today's terms). Furnishing was not a problem – there were plenty of wedding presents which fitted perfectly.

Right: Princess Elizabeth, on her first official overseas visit to France in May 1948, chats to Mme Bidault, wife of the French Prime Minister, Georges Bidault, at the Palace of Versailles.

But the pace of life slowed when their first son, Charles Philip Arthur George, was born on 14 November 1948 at Buckingham Palace, almost a year to the day since they were married. Elizabeth and Philip finally settled down to domestic happiness with their baby in Clarence House in July 1949, relishing space they could call their own. And when the Duke of Edinburgh was posted to Malta in October to join HMS *Chequers* as first lieutenant, his wife flew out to join him on two occasions, each time staying for several weeks. Baby Charles stayed behind with his grandparents.

Here was the perfect life for a young married couple. The Princess could shop, meet friends and throw parties at the Villa Guardamangia, the house on the outskirts of Valetta loaned to them by Earl Mountbatten. Just like any other navy wife she could enjoy picnics and beach parties.

When she returned to England in the spring of 1950 she was expecting her second child, Princess Anne, who was born on 15 August.

Right: Princess Elizabeth watches over her month-old baby son, Charles, in December 1948.

The infant Prince Charles, dressed in a family gown of Honiton lace, was christened by the Archbishop of Canterbury in the Music Room at Buckingham Palace on 15 December 1948. He was held throughout the ceremony by the youngest godmother, his proud aunt, Princess Margaret, then 18 years old. Only Prince Charles himself seemed unhappy, bawling loudly when a barrage of photographers' lights flashed, but he was soon pacified with a silver rattle.

Left: Prince Charles, with his parents, after his christening at Buckingham Palace in December 1948.

Above: Less than a year before Princess Elizabeth was to become Queen: she and her husband, the Duke of Edinburgh, are pictured holding their young children, Anne and Charles.

An Ailing King

The only dark cloud was the state of the King's health. An operation to relieve hardening of the arteries meant that he had to take life a lot more easily. But it was clear he welcomed the birth of another grandchild and was delighted when Philip became lieutenant-commander, in charge of the frigate *Magpie*. When Princess Anne was three months old, the Duke of Edinburgh flew to Gibraltar to represent the King at the opening of the Legislative Assembly. His wife joined him and together they made a semi-official visit to Greece, sailing across the Ionian Sea and enjoying a rapturous reception in Athens.

Back home, Clarence House had become a family home and a haven from increasingly frequent public engagements. King George managed to open the Festival of Britain, a huge 'trade show' marking the country's recovery from war, in May 1951, but he was clearly unwell. By autumn a diagnosis of lung cancer was made and although he came through the necessary operation his daughter and son-in-law were to represent him on a tour of Canada and the United States.

The young couple broke with royal tradition and flew together to Canada, arriving on 8 October for their month-long coast-to-coast trip. Princess Elizabeth, with Philip keeping her spirits up, relaxed and was able to put anxieties about her father to one side as ball followed banquet, inspections, presentations and speeches, even square dancing and a visit to the famous Calgary Stampede. By comparison the three-day visit to the USA as guests of President Truman passed in a flash.

Their son, Charles, who had just celebrated his third birthday, and 15-month-old toddler Anne were waiting at home for their parents – as was another round of engagements and ceremony. Respite came at Christmas when the family, including King George, happy to have his daughters and grandchildren with him, enjoyed a peaceful holiday at Sandringham.

On the last day of January 1952 the King stood on the tarmac at London Airport, waving to his daughter and son-in-law as they embarked on the BOAC aircraft *Atlanta* for an extensive tour, in his name, to East Africa, Australia and New Zealand.

They were not to see him again. Less than one week later he died peacefully in his sleep and his beloved daughter, just 25 years old, became Her Majesty Queen Elizabeth II.

Worry in 1951 about the failing health of King George VI was so real that Princess Elizabeth carried with her to Canada a sealed envelope containing the draft of her accession declaration, just in case he died while she was away. She did not have to open it on that occasion.

Above: Princess Elizabeth enjoys a carefree interlude at a square dance in Ottawa on an official visit to Canada in 1951.

Left: King George VI waves goodbye to Princess Elizabeth as she and her husband leave for their Commonwealth Tour in 1952. She was not to see her father again.

There had been misgivings from some in Canada before the five-week tour, but by the time the royal couple made their farewells, the country had been won over. The news of their triumph came home before them, and the King showed his pleasure by making both Elizabeth and Philip members of the Privy Council.

LONG LIVE *The Queen*

The hot sunshine, colourful ceremonies, exotic sights and sounds, and a photographic safari in Nairobi National Park – where Elizabeth, a dab hand with a camera, took pictures of giraffe, zebra and a handsome lion – seemed a good start to the East Africa visit.

The people of Kenya had given the couple a small house, Sagana Lodge, on the lower slopes of Mount Kenya, as a wedding present and there they relaxed for a few days before visiting Treetops, a cabin built high in giant fig trees over a drinking hole where wild animals, illuminated by moonlight, came at night and could be observed in safety at close quarters. Here the Duke and Duchess of Edinburgh spent the night, standing entranced on the balcony as rhino, elephant and waterbuck came down to the pool to drink. They returned to Sagana Lodge where, in the early afternoon of 6 February, Prince Philip broke the sad news to Princess Elizabeth that her father had died in the night.

She had little time to grieve. Within an hour the new Queen was packed and ready to fly home. She and Philip had been married just four years and three months – and much of that time had been spent discharging royal duties and engagements. Now the rest of their days were mapped out.

Right: Princess Elizabeth attends a polo match in Kenya, in February 1952.

Below: Sagana Hunting Lodge, Nyeri, Kenya, where Prince Philip broke the news of her father's death to the new Queen.

Prime Minister Winston Churchill was waiting by the runway at London Airport on the evening of 7 February as Her Majesty Queen Elizabeth II, her small figure dwarfed by the huge aircraft, walked down its steps to be greeted.

A hastily erected Royal Standard fluttered over Clarence House as she and the Duke of Edinburgh arrived home. The next day she made her accession declaration at St James's Palace.

'By the sudden death of my dear father I am called to assume the duties and responsibilities of sovereignty,' she said. 'My heart is too full for me to say more to you today than I shall always work, as my father did throughout his reign, to advance the happiness and prosperity of my peoples, spread as they are all the world over.'

The first to pay homage to the young Queen was her grandmother, Queen Mary, who was driven through the dusk from Marlborough House to Clarence House to greet her with a curtsy and kiss her hand as a 'Grannie and subject'.

Left: The slight figure of Queen Elizabeth II descends from the aircraft to be greeted by (right to left) Winston Churchill, Clement Attlee, Anthony Eden and Frederick Marquis, the Earl of Woolton, on her return from Kenya.

However sad the news, however stricken by grief, The Queen has been taught since childhood that she is always in the public view. She rarely lets private emotion show. In the eyes of the world she is the figurehead for her people and, as such, her public face must be composed and serene. Elizabeth, the daughter, grieving for a beloved father, had to hide her sorrow and do what she knew was her duty. The famously waspish *Daily Mirror* columnist William Connor, who wrote under the pseudonym 'Cassandra', had sympathized with the Royal Family's lot in March 1951. He wrote of the 'unyielding routine that is the lot of British Royalty – the endless timeless, remorseless duty of always being on parade'.

THE *Coronation*

The 86-year-old Queen Mary, wife to King George V, mother to the next two monarchs and grandmother to the new Queen, was not present at the funeral of her son, King George VI. She had already lost her husband and two sons, and now a third, the dutiful and loving Bertie, was dead too. Feeling unable to attend the funeral, she watched the cortège as it passed by her window in Marlborough House and reflected that soon her granddaughter, Elizabeth, for whom she had high hopes, would be crowned Queen.

Sadly Queen Mary did not live to see the coronation, dying just 10 weeks before, on 24 March 1953. Her instructions had been that the occasion should not be postponed in the event of her death.

And so it was that on 2 June 1953 crowds, once again camped out along the coronation route, received a dousing from the British weather, but no one grumbled as the long and colourful procession marched, precisely on time and in time at 112 paces a minute, to the ceremony in Westminster Abbey.

In the year before her coronation, The Queen performed her new ceremonial duties with a skill and grace that delighted many. She held her first investiture just three weeks after the accession and distributed 25 pieces of Maundy money (one for each year of her age) at Westminster Abbey on the Thursday before Easter. There was the State Opening of Parliament and another birthday inspection of the Grenadier Guards, but the biggest plaudits came when she became the first reigning Queen since her namesake, Queen Elizabeth I, to ride at the head of her military cavalcade for Trooping the Colour on 5 June.

Above: The Queen carries out the first engagement of her reign – distribution of the Royal Maundy at Westminster Abbey. Here she walks past a line of Yeomen of the Guard.

Left: The Queen arrives at Westminster Abbey wearing her coronation robes and crown. She is accompanied by her husband, the Duke of Edinburgh and her Maids of Honour.

Below: A solemn moment during the coronation ceremony on 2 June 1953.

The Queen's coronation took place in the early days of television, when few families owned their own set. Television cameras had never before been allowed inside Westminster Abbey, and the Coronation Joint Executive and the Cabinet had decided against it for this occasion. When Prime Minister Winston Churchill told The Queen in October 1952 of the unanimous decision of her advisors, she reminded him that it was she who was being crowned, not the Cabinet. She felt that all her subjects should have the opportunity to see the event. In Britain, more than 20 million people, crowded around small television sets in neighbours' front rooms, watched as the young Queen was crowned.

First came the Lord Mayor of London (Sir Rupert de la Bère) and his procession, and then the Speaker of the House of Commons (William Morrison), each in his own coach. Some members of the Royal Family were driven in motor cars, as were representatives of 72 countries. Carriage processions followed – colonial rulers, and princes and princesses of the 'royal blood'. Everyone was on tiptoe, eager to catch a glimpse of the Queen Mother and Princess Margaret, together in the Glass Coach.

Then it was the time for the most colourful part of the procession: at 10.26 a.m. precisely the Gold State Coach, drawn by eight Windsor Greys, bearing The Queen, with the Duke of Edinburgh at her side, left Buckingham Palace. Bewigged postilions and footmen, the Yeomen of the Guard, four divisions of the Sovereign's Escort, The Queen's Bargemaster and 12 Watermen accompanied the horses, while the coach was flanked by mounted officers – the Master of the Horse, the Lord High Constable, Gold-Stick-in-Waiting, Silver-Stick-in-Waiting, personal aides-de-camp and equerries.

The magnificent progress was led by a mounted officer, four troopers of the Household Cavalry, five companies of Foot Guards, the bands and corps of the Irish and Welsh Guards, five more companies of Foot Guards and the Kings' Troop, Royal Horse Artillery.

This coronation was the first to be televised and millions the world over watched as The Queen, seated on the Chair of Estate, took the Coronation Oath, administered by the Archbishop of Canterbury, Dr Geoffrey Francis Fisher.

Below: The Queen, her family and attendants greet the crowds from Buckingham Palace balcony after the coronation ceremony.

Above: Queen Elizabeth II, carrying the orb and sceptre and wearing the Imperial State Crown, enters Buckingham Palace following her coronation.

THE QUEEN *at Home*

Having spent the first happy years of marriage at Clarence House, neither The Queen nor her husband viewed the necessary move to Buckingham Palace with any great joy. Now the Queen Mother and Princess Margaret would make Clarence House their home, while the royal couple and their children were, in the Duke of Edinburgh's words, to move back to the 'museum', their own 'tied cottage'. But they ensured that their private apartments were, in contrast to the 19 magnificent state rooms, comfortable and homely, and it was here that the couple's two youngest children, Andrew and Edward, were born in 1960 and 1964 respectively.

Many who come to stand and gaze at Buckingham Palace and Windsor Castle know that when the Royal Standard – the official flag of the reigning monarch – flutters overhead, The Queen is in residence. The Union flag is flown when she is not there.

Royal Residences

Although Buckingham Palace is her official home, it is widely acknowledged that **Windsor Castle**, the largest occupied castle in the world, is The Queen's favourite residence. As youngsters, Princess Elizabeth and her sister were evacuated here in 1940, remaining for the duration of the Second World War, and enjoying spending much of their time at nearby Royal Lodge. Today The Queen undertakes formal duties at Windsor, especially the hosting of state visits and the annual Order of the Garter ceremony – but at just over 20 miles (32km) outside London, it provides the perfect weekend retreat where she and her family can relax and enjoy leisure activities including riding, carriage-driving, polo and shooting. Windsor is where The Queen and the Duke stay for a month over Easter each year, and for a week in June when she attends the Royal Ascot race meeting. They also spend part of the Christmas period here. Despite its vastness – the Castle alone covers 13 acres (5ha), and it is set within the Great Park's 5,700 acres (2,300ha) – it is very much a home.

But **Buckingham Palace** remains The Queen's main residence; along with Windsor Castle and the Palace of Holyroodhouse in Edinburgh, it does not belong to the Royal Family but to the nation. Buckingham Palace in particular has magnificent state apartments filled with priceless works of art – also state-owned and many on display in the adjoining Queen's Gallery.

Balmoral in Scotland and Sandringham in Norfolk, however, both belong to The Queen. These two massive country estates were left by her father, who had bought them from his brother, King Edward VIII, when he abdicated in 1936. 'In London I have a house; at Sandringham I have a home,' said The Queen's grandfather, King George V, who also stated it was the place he loved best in the world. Both George V and George VI died peacefully at Sandringham. Summer holidays through August and September at Balmoral, and a family Christmas at Sandringham, where The Queen can enjoy her favourite country pursuits, have always been treasured escapes from the public eye.

Above: The magnificent front of Buckingham Palace.

Left: A sweep of lawn in the grounds leads to this view of Windsor Castle not generally seen by the public.

In Scotland, picnics, walking, fishing and deer-stalking are enjoyed – whatever the weather. **Balmoral Castle**, set in its 11,000-acre (4,450-ha) estate, was bought in 1852 by Queen Victoria, the great-great-grandmother Queen Elizabeth admires so much. Balmoral, inside and out, has a Victorian feel, with heavy furniture of the period and a lot of tartan in evidence. For all that, The Queen and Prince Philip have introduced a more informal atmosphere which recreates the happy memories she has of family holidays spent here with her parents and sister.

Today her own children and grandchildren join the family party and, during the eight-week stay, other guests – including old friends, government ministers and foreign dignitaries – are invited to enjoy Balmoral, but are expected to arrive well-prepared for outdoor activities. They are guided in their choice of wardrobe by the daily programme, organized by the Duke of Edinburgh. Every September the Prime Minister and spouse spend a long weekend, Friday to Sunday, at Balmoral – mixing a little business with varying degrees of pleasure, depending on the guests' enjoyment of the great outdoors. Winston Churchill, Harold Wilson and James Callaghan all thoroughly

Below: The Royal Standard announces The Queen's presence as it flutters from a turret at Balmoral.

Originally a monastery founded in 1128, the Palace of Holyroodhouse in Edinburgh is The Queen's official residence in Scotland. It was here in the grounds in 1938 that The Queen's grandparents, King George V and Queen Mary, hosted the first garden party, a tradition that continues to this day.

Below: The Palace of Holyroodhouse, residence of kings and queens since the 15th century.

The great hall at Balmoral is besieged by bats roosting under the high ceiling. The Queen, with the help of a footman and a long-handled net, likes to catch them before releasing them outside. But these protected creatures are soon back again, ready to face another session with the royal net.

enjoyed themselves while Margaret Thatcher was not so keen on country life, although her husband, Denis, was in his element.

The Queen is Laird of Balmoral and, as such, is a guest of honour at many local events, including the Braemar Gathering, of which she is the Chieftain. She rarely fails to attend these Highland Games, the biggest in Scotland, where pipers and dancers entertain the crowds who have come to watch traditional activities such as tossing the caber, putting the stone and throwing the hammer.

The Queen is known to enjoy Scottish country dancing, and during her stay at Balmoral she hosts dances known as Gillies' Balls for neighbours, staff and people living locally.

A small and solitary house on the banks of Loch Muick, built for Queen Victoria, marks a favourite picnic spot for The Queen and her family in Scotland. Family and guests – and dogs – pile into a couple of four-wheel-drive vehicles, one driven by The Queen, loaded with picnic baskets and wet-weather gear. They set off on tracks through the heather to enjoy a day spent walking, fishing and eating food often cooked on a barbecue or fire by Prince Philip.

Left: The Queen and Prince Philip relax in the Drawing Room at Balmoral, a corgi at their feet.

Right: Prince Charles shares a joke with his mother during the Braemar Highland Games in September 2010.

Christmas at Sandringham

The baby Princess Elizabeth was eight months old when she was first taken to **Sandringham** in December 1926 to spend Christmas with her maternal grandparents. She grew to love this country estate in north Norfolk as much as her father and grandfather had done.

The Queen, Prince Philip, their children and grandchildren continue to come together at Sandringham each year for a traditional Christmas – although many of the traditions are their own. There is always a 20-ft (6-m) tall Christmas tree, cut from the estate and decorated by The Queen, in pride of place in the White Drawing Room. By the tree are trestle tables, draped in spotless white linen cloths, with name cards showing where presents are to be piled.

The Royal Family follows the tradition of many Europeans, opening presents on Christmas Eve – but not before enjoying a get-together over tea, laid out on sideboards in the Saloon, the imposing entrance hall. When the sandwiches, scones and cakes have been eaten and the tea drunk, the family gathers around the tree for a present-opening session – the rule being that the gifts, except for the children who receive large stockings full of exciting toys, are inexpensive and practical.

Sandringham was bought in 1862 for the then Prince of Wales, Prince Albert Edward, later King Edward VII. The estate now extends to around 20,000 acres (8,000ha) and is famous for its shooting. Its first owner enjoyed the sport and the outdoor life so much that he established 'Sandringham Time' – the clocks on the estate being kept half-an-hour fast, so that the most could be made of daylight hours. The practice was abolished on the death of George V in 1936.

Below: Sandringham House in Norfolk, the setting for the Royal Family's Christmas celebrations.

Then it is time to dress for a black-tie dinner, preceded by gins-and-tonic and dry martinis in the Saloon before going in to a candlelit dinner. Beautiful china and shining silverware are laid on the table which is decorated with flowers and greenery from the estate. The Queen's corgis, never far away, sit in a corner of the room. Dinner may consist of Norfolk seafood followed by local lamb or game and a pudding such as tarte tatin with brandy cream. When The Queen gives the signal, the corgis are led out and the ladies adjourn, as Prince Philip serves port or brandy to the men.

There are stockings full of small presents for everyone before breakfast, after which the Royal Family is 'on parade' for the Christmas Day service held at St Mary Magdalene church. Outside are crowds who have been gathering since early morning to catch a glimpse of – or maybe a chance to speak with – their favourite royal. Estate-bred turkey is served for lunch, after which the whole family settles down in front of a crackling log fire to watch The Queen's Christmas Message on television.

Right: Members of the public step forward to greet the Royal Family after the Christmas Day church service at Sandringham in 2010.

History was made on Christmas Day 1932 when King George V made the first live Christmas broadcast by radio 'to the Empire' from Sandringham: it lasted 2½ minutes. His granddaughter continues the tradition, although today The Queen's Christmas Message, broadcast on television, is pre-recorded and informal. It still goes out at 3 p.m. as is customary, chosen originally as the hour best suited to reaching most countries in the British Empire by short-wave transmission.

Right: In December 1952, The Queen makes her first Christmas broadcast from Sandringham.

THE SPORT of Queens

The young Elizabeth loved horses and was allowed to learn to ride at an early age. She is now acknowledged as an expert on breeding racehorses and as an owner with an eye for potential in a horse. Her first win came early on when Astrakhan, a filly given as a wedding present by the Aga Khan, romped home to win at Hurst Park in 1949.

Now her racing interests are run as a business, managed for years by her old friend the late 7th Earl of Carnarvon. As Lord Porchester he would escort Princess Elizabeth to Epsom, Newmarket and Ascot. He became her racing manager in 1969 and together they saw her runners win all the major races – except the Derby, last won by a royal horse (owned by Edward VII) in 1909. Horses like Highclere and Dunfermline have won the 1,000 Guineas and the Prix de Diane, the Oaks and St Leger.

The Queen, who has around 25 horses in training at any one time, lost not only an astute manager but also a valued and trusted friend when Lord Carnarvon died suddenly in 2001. His son-in-law, John Warren, took over her racing interests.

The Queen's mares are kept at the Royal Stud at Sandringham which is run successfully thanks to her enthusiasm for breeding and racing. When a mare foals, she receives all the details, including a photograph, and follows each foal's development keenly.

The Royal racing colours are gold-braided purple body with scarlet sleeves and a black velvet cap with a gold fringe; these are the colours she will be cheering when she attends race meetings as an owner and breeder, and in an official capacity at events which enjoy Royal patronage, such as the Derby and Royal Ascot. She is often accompanied by her children and grandchildren who have inherited her love for the sport.

There was disappointment for The Queen in 2011 when her talented young horse Carlton House, tipped to win the Derby – a prize that has eluded the Royal family for more than a century – came in third.

Right: The Queen canters to the start of a race at Royal Ascot in June 1961.

Dogs have long been favoured pets of the Royal Family as portraits going back to the 17th century, showing royals enjoying the company of their faithful friends, confirm. When George VI bought his first corgi, called Dookie, he felt it had 'unquestionably the character of a princess' and to this day that breed has been first choice for the family. The Queen's love of this breed of dog has been evident since childhood, and the newly married Duchess of Edinburgh even took her favourite corgi, Susan (an 18th-birthday gift), with her on honeymoon. Where she goes, the corgis go too – as do her 'dorgis' – a cross between the corgi and the dachshund.

Above: The Queen and the Duke of Edinburgh arrive at Ascot Racecourse by carriage in June 2011.

The Queen's passion for breeding and owning racehorses is well known. But pigeon fancying? Her Majesty takes a keen interest in the royal pigeon lofts at Sandringham where the descendents of birds given to the Royal Family by King Leopold II of Belgium in 1886 regularly win races. During both world wars the Sandringham pigeons were used, successfully, to carry messages.

Left: Pigeon post is the method used by the two young Princesses, Elizabeth and Margaret, to send a message to the Chief Guide, Lady Olave Baden-Powell, in 1943.

THE QUEEN *at Work*

The Queen's day starts early, when a maid, nodding 'good morning' to the police security guard in the corridor, taps on the bedroom door, entering the pale green room bearing a tray of Earl Grey tea. She draws the curtains and switches on the radio, tuned to the BBC Radio 4 *Today* programme, before running Her Majesty's bath. Meanwhile the first outfit of the day – depending on her schedule, The Queen may have to change as many as five times – is laid out in the dressing room. Prince Philip is also getting ready for the day ahead in his next-door suite of rooms, comprising bedroom, library, bathroom, dressing room and office.

Buckingham Palace is their main home – but also their workplace. The couple have adjoining offices where they adjourn after breakfast, which is served at 8.30 a.m. in The Queen's private dining room, often to the accompaniment of bagpipe music from The Queen's Piper playing on the terrace below the window.

By 9.30 a.m. The Queen is at work in her office, which doubles as a sitting room, with comfortable armchairs and sofas. The predominant colour is green, and fresh flowers have been arranged earlier by the Palace florist. The Queen, accompanied by her corgis, heads for the Chippendale desk, which came with her from Clarence House 60 years ago. The many objects on the desk include a thick-nibbed fountain pen, a double inkwell and a thick sheet of blotting paper – black, like the ink, so that it cannot be read. Every day there are at least 200 letters to be answered. These have already been filtered and most are dealt with by a lady-in-waiting. The Queen decides which need a personal reply.

There are on average two investitures held each month at Buckingham Palace. These ceremonies always start at 11 a.m. in the State Ballroom where The Queen, or another senior member of the Royal Family, presents Orders, decorations and medals.

Left: All in a day's work: The Queen receives Jadranka Negodic, Ambassador of Bosnia and Herzegovina, at Buckingham Palace in February 2009.

Right: An elegant Queen Elizabeth arrives at a royal film performance in Leicester Square in 1952.

Privy Council meetings, held in the late afternoons and attended by The Queen, happen monthly. Business is conducted standing up – a practice initiated by Queen Victoria as a mark of respect when her beloved husband, Prince Albert, died in 1861.

Then the famous 'red boxes' arrive with Her Majesty's private secretary. Inside are documents and papers, letters and telegrams from Government ministers and Commonwealth officials. They must all be read, and, if necessary, signed. 'Meeting and greeting' follows: ambassadors, high-ranking newly appointed (or just retired) members of the armed forces, new bishops and judges will have a 10-minute audience, usually alone, with The Queen in a separate room near her office; she may meet eminent prize-winning writers or scientists, to present their awards.

Lunch is generally a private affair, followed by a quiet half-hour when The Queen likes to walk her dogs in the Palace gardens, giving her time to think through any problems

Once a week she holds a confidential meeting with the Prime Minister, normally on a Wednesday and always at 6.30 p.m. An hour later, a 'Today in Parliament' report is emailed over and she makes a point of reading this before bedtime. The remainder of the evening might be spent hosting a reception or dinner, or she may go out, in her official capacity, to a concert, film première or as guest of an organization of which she is a patron or president.

If there is time to relax, Her Majesty settles down to solve crosswords or giant jigsaws before bed at around 11 p.m.

Sometimes The Queen spends the morning on engagements, visiting up to three venues, either alone or with the Duke of Edinburgh. She carries out around 430 engagements each year, opening buildings and events, unveiling plaques and making speeches. Afternoon engagements are more usual, to, for example, hospitals, factories, schools, community schemes, military units and art galleries. She travels by helicopter or an RAF aircraft if the visit is outside London. A longer visit normally entails overnight travel on the Royal Train.

The Family FIRM

P rince Philip likens the job of the Royal Family to that of a business. With characteristic bluntness he calls the senior members 'The Firm' – a term first used by The Queen's father, King George VI.

The Queen and her husband have, in the course of 65 years of marriage, formed an enduring partnership, professionally and privately, each complementing the other. His naval career was brought abruptly to a halt in 1952 when his wife acceded to the throne; it cannot have been easy for this intelligent and forthright man of action to forgo his own ambitions in the interests of The Queen and the nation. But he has not only supported his wife in her royal duties, he has also carved out a career of his own, heading more than 800 organizations as their patron or president, carrying out many solo overseas visits in support of British business, overseeing his Duke of Edinburgh Award Scheme set up in 1959, and ensuring that the Royal residences and estates are run efficiently and profitably.

The Queen's Children

The heir to the throne, **Prince Charles**, the Prince of Wales and his wife Camilla, Duchess of Cornwall carry out hundreds of engagements at home and abroad each year. The Prince is a champion of the arts, music and environmental causes. He and the Duchess oversee the work of the Prince's Trust, set up in 1979 to help young people. In April 2011 the Trust merged with another youth charity, Fairbridge. Prince Charles is an enthusiastic gardener and promotes organic principles at his Highgrove House garden in Gloucestershire and on the Duchy farms, mostly in south-west England, which produce high-quality food and drink.

Left: Prince Charles, Prince of Wales and Camilla, Duchess of Cornwall meet volunteers from the Youth United network in Croydon, August 2011.

Above: Princess Anne, the Princess Royal meets military veterans at a Buckingham Palace Garden Party in July 2011.

Right: Prince Andrew, Duke of York (left) and his brother, Prince Edward, Earl of Wessex walking to the Easter service at St George's Chapel, Windsor, in April 2011.

Princess Anne, the Princess Royal, is 10th in line to the throne. She is as well known for her sporting prowess as an international Eventing champion as for her engagements, which number around 600 each year. In 1976 she became the only member of the Royal Family to have won a place in the British Olympic Team, and is now President of the British Olympic Association and a UK member of the International Olympic Committee. She takes on many official engagements on behalf of her mother, and works on behalf of approximately 200 charities.

Prince Andrew, fourth in line to the royal Crown, served in the Royal Navy where he trained as a helicopter pilot, and holds the rank of Commander. On his 50th birthday in 2010 he was made an honorary Rear Admiral. He saw active service during the Falklands War of 1982 – he and his father, along with nephew Prince Harry, are the only living members of the Royal Family to have served under direct enemy fire.

Prince Edward, the royal couple's fourth and last child, is seventh in the line of succession. He achieved a university degree at Cambridge, having read history at Jesus College. After a short time in the Royal Marines, he moved into theatre where his career desires truly lay. As the Earl and Countess of Wessex, he and his wife, Sophie, take on many royal duties on behalf of The Queen and the Duke of Edinburgh.

One of the lowest points for the whole Royal Family must have been the terrible fire that ravaged Windsor Castle in 1992, the year The Queen called her *annus horribilis* (year of horrors). But she must have relished entering the magnificently restored St George's Hall at the Castle five years later to celebrate her Golden Wedding anniversary. She and the Duke of Edinburgh, partners in everything they have done through life, have since celebrated their Diamond Wedding anniversary – and in 2012 their Blue Sapphire (65th) anniversary – and still work together, bound by mutual love, respect and understanding.

Like everyone else, The Queen knows the great joys and deep sorrows of life. Her Majesty, 86 years old in her Jubilee year, has lived through war and a society that has changed more rapidly than at any other time in history. She has experienced the joy of her own long and happy marriage, of family life with four children, eight grandchildren and, at the time of her Diamond Jubilee, one great-granddaughter. But she has also seen three of her children's marriages fail and, with the rest of the nation, experienced the shock of the tragic death of Diana, Princess of Wales in Paris in August 1997.

In 2002 the people of Britain, with a spontaneous outpouring of affection and respect, celebrated her Golden Jubilee, thronging The Mall and cheering with undiluted enthusiasm as she and Prince Philip appeared on Buckingham Palace balcony. Many of her subjects met her during that year as she toured the length and breadth of the country, shaking hands and chatting to those who flocked to greet her.

Earlier that year her beloved mother, Queen Elizabeth the Queen Mother, and her younger sister, Margaret, to whom she was devoted, had both died, so that a year which began with great sadness, ended on a high note.

In April 2011 the nation celebrated as her grandson, Prince William, now the Duke of Cambridge, married his long-time sweetheart, Catherine Middleton, in a moving ceremony at Westminster Abbey. William's grandmother, The Queen, looked as happy and relaxed as the young couple themselves.

Above: The Queen invests her son, Prince Charles, as Prince of Wales.

The Queen carries out hundreds of investitures every year but the most special was on 1 July 1969, when her son, 20-year-old Prince Charles, was invested as the 21st Prince of Wales. The ancient walls of Caernarfon Castle were the setting for the ceremony where she handed the regalia to her eldest child as he knelt before her.

Left: 4 June 2002: a colourful parade along The Mall, led by The Queen and the Duke of Edinburgh, marks her Golden Jubilee year.

Above: The Duke and Duchess of Cambridge visit Calgary Zoo in Canada on their first joint overseas tour, July 2011.

The newest Royal Family 'team' is that of the Duke and Duchess of Cambridge – Prince William and his wife Catherine. They married to public acclaim in April 2011, an occasion which showed the Royal Family at its most relaxed and happy. The Duke and Duchess made their first official trip together just over two months after their marriage, when they toured Canada and visited the USA for a few days. Prince William is second in line to the throne, after his father, Prince Charles, so one day, like The Queen and the Duke of Edinburgh, he and his wife will head up 'The Firm'.

THE *Season*

Every year The Queen and other members of the Royal Family are guests of honour or hosts at events which have become high spots of the summer season.

The **Chelsea Flower Show**, each May, has been a regular fixture in the royal calendar since it was first held in 1913 in the grounds of the Royal Hospital, Chelsea. The Queen, as Patron of the Royal Horticultural Society, and often accompanied by other members of the Royal Family, regularly attends the opening of the show.

The summer season would be incomplete without The Queen's **Garden Parties**, three at Buckingham Palace and one at Holyroodhouse in Edinburgh. Each year up to 40,000 people from all walks of life receive a special invitation. This is the only occasion when honoured members of the public have a chance to view the Palace gardens with their well-stocked flower beds, lakes, statues and garden sculpture, and pretty summer house. Sandwiches, bridge rolls, tea, coffee and cakes are served. The Queen and the Duke of Edinburgh and other senior members of the Royal Family are present at these relaxed and informal gatherings where guests are entertained by two bands.

The week that spans the end of June and beginning of July is when The Queen and the Duke of Edinburgh visit Scotland to celebrate its culture, history and achievement. **Holyrood Week** always begins with the Ceremony of the Keys, where The Queen is received by Edinburgh's City Chamberlain, given the keys of the city and welcomed to 'your ancient and hereditary kingdom of Scotland'. She holds investitures in the Great Gallery of the Palace of Holyroodhouse and – the Duke of Edinburgh at her side – welcomes guests to her annual **Garden Party**.

The Diamond Jubilee year also sees the 100th anniversary of the Royal Variety Performance. The Queen and the Prince of Wales take turns to be guest of honour at the annual event which raises money for retired entertainers through the Entertainment Artistes' Benevolent Fund (EABF). It is a glittering occasion – first attended by King George V and Queen Mary in 1912 at London's Palace Theatre in Piccadilly Circus. Other charities with long royal associations include Barnardo's and Save the Children Fund.

Left: The Queen meets guests at a special party for underprivileged children, held in the grounds of Buckingham Palace.

With her passion for horse racing, The Queen is known to enjoy the annual Meeting at **Royal Ascot** in June. Stylish hats and sleek racehorses are the order of the day at this racecourse founded by Queen Anne in 1711. Queen Elizabeth has had 20 winners at Ascot to date. Each day begins, by long tradition, with the arrival of The Queen and the royal party in horse-drawn landaus. The exclusive heart of the meeting is the Royal Enclosure, where entry is gained only by sponsorship from an existing member who has attended at least four times before. Here gentlemen must wear morning dress with a top hat, and ladies are required to dress in formal day-wear. Ascot's most famous race is The Gold Cup, run over a 2 mile and 4 furlong (4,023m) course; the race was inaugurated in 1807, with a prize of 100 guineas.

A special display at Chelsea in 1937 was created to celebrate the coronation of The Queen's father, King George VI. The imaginative exhibits focussed on plants representing different parts of the Commonwealth.

Right: Enjoying the floral displays at the Chelsea Flower Show in May 2011.

Below: The Ceremony of the Keys marks the start of an annual round of royal engagements in Scotland. Here The Queen inspects a Guard of Honour during the ceremony in 2010.

STATE OCCASIONS & *Ceremonies*

There are many occasions during the year when The Queen, as Head of State, performs duties whose origins have great historical significance.

The most colourful and important event of the Parliamentary year is the **State Opening of Parliament**, when the Houses of Lords and Commons and the Crown come together. The Queen travels to the Palace of Westminster in a State Coach – but only after a couple of precautions have been taken. A detachment of the Yeomen of the Guard searches the cellars, to ensure there is no Gunpowder Plot in the offing, and then a Member of Parliament, usually a Government whip, is held 'hostage' at Buckingham Palace to ensure Her Majesty's safe return. This custom dates from times when hostilities existed between the Crown and Parliament.

Four historic bodyguards attend the Sovereign at ceremonial occasions such as the State Opening of Parliament. Her Majesty's Body Guard of the Honourable Corps of Gentlemen at Arms, The Queen's Body Guard of the Yeomen of the Guard, Yeomen Warders and, in Scotland, the Royal Company of Archers, all have a long history of colourful tradition.

The Imperial State Crown, travelling ahead of The Queen, in its own carriage, is escorted by Members of the Royal Household. Once in the House of Lords, The Queen dons the crown and her crimson parliamentary robe. Then Black Rod, the Queen's Messenger, knocks on the door of the House of Commons to summon MPs to attend the ceremony. The door is opened – and instantly slammed in Black Rod's face. It is then reopened to enable Black Rod to convey the Sovereign's summons. This is a reminder of the right of the Commons to exclude everyone but the Sovereign's messengers. No monarch has set foot in the Commons since Charles I entered in 1642 and tried to arrest five Members.

Remembrance Day is a solemn occasion when – at the 11th hour of the 11th day of the 11th month – the nation pays homage to those who died in two world wars and other conflicts. On Remembrance Sunday – the nearest Sunday to 11 November – The Queen, other members of the Royal Family and political party leaders join representatives of the Armed Forces and ex-servicemen and women for the two-minute silence and the 'Last Post'. Her Majesty leads the others in laying her wreath of poppies at the Cenotaph in Whitehall.

Above: In 2010, a solemn Queen Elizabeth prepares to lay a wreath at the Cenotaph in London during the annual Remembrance Sunday ceremony; Prime Minister, David Cameron, and Deputy Prime Minister, Nick Clegg, can be seen in the background.

Left: The Queen and Prince Philip process through the Royal Gallery in the Palace of Westminster during the State Opening of Parliament on 25 May 2010.

A group of six traditional rowing skiffs travel the River Thames between Sunbury Lock and Abingdon for five days each July in order to determine the health of the swan population. As the cry 'All up!' rings out, the Royal Swan Uppers row towards families of swans, lifting the cygnets out of the water to weigh and measure them and check their health. They are accompanied by The Queen's Swan Marker and the Swan Uppers of the Vintners and Dyers Livery Companies who, like The Queen, exercise their right of ownership of these stately birds on the river. These customs date back to the 12th century when swans were regarded as tasty fare.

More than 400 years ago the colours, or flags, of the battalion were 'trooped' down the ranks, so that in time of battle they would be recognized by all the soldiers. **Trooping the Colour** has traditionally marked the Sovereign's official birthday and since 1901 the reigning monarch has taken the salute in person at the ceremony. Although Her Majesty was born in April, it is customary for the Sovereign's official birthday to be held in June, when the weather is deemed to be better.

The Queen, then Princess Elizabeth, took her first salute in 1951, when her father, King George VI, was too ill to do so. Mounted side-saddle on a well-trained police horse she sat ramrod straight as she saluted. The Queen has attended Trooping the Colour every year of her reign, except 1955 when a national rail strike forced cancellation. For many years she rode her favourite mare, Burmese, in the parade but they both retired from that activity in 1986. Now she arrives at Horse Guards for the two-hour ceremony in a phaeton built for Queen Victoria.

The **Garter Ceremony** has its origins even further back. The Order of the Garter, the oldest British Order of Chivalry, was founded by Edward III in 1348. 'Garter Day', with its colourful procession and service, happens in June, on the Monday of Royal Ascot week. On that day any new Companions are invested with the insignia by Her

Far left: The Queen, flanked by Prince Philip (right) and Prince Charles, takes part in Trooping the Colour in 1980.

Left: Wearing traditional robes, The Queen and the Duke of Edinburgh share a smile as they walk in procession to St George's Chapel, Windsor, on 13 June 2011 for the annual Order of the Garter ceremony.

Right: Her Majesty celebrates her 85th birthday on 21 April 2011 by distributing the Royal Maundy to elderly people at Westminster Abbey.

Majesty in the Throne Room of Windsor Castle before she hosts a lunch in the Waterloo Chamber. After lunch the Knights, wearing blue velvet 'mantels' or robes and white-plumed black velvet hats, are led on foot by the Constable and Governor of Windsor Castle and the Military Knights of Windsor to St George's Chapel for a short service, before returning to the Castle by carriage. The Queen and the Duke of Edinburgh attend the service with other members of the Royal Family in the Order.

Early in her reign The Queen decided that the **Royal Maundy** presentation on the Thursday before Easter should take place in a different British cathedral or abbey each year. The presentation of silver coins, in white and red purses, is made to elderly people in recognition of their services to the community. Traditionally the number of coins and recipients matches the age of the Sovereign. At Westminster Abbey in 2011, for example, 85 men and 85 women each received two purses – a white one containing 85p in Maundy coins and a red one with a £5 coin and a 50p piece.

State Visits
& OVERSEAS TOURS

In her 60 years on the throne, Her Majesty, as Head of State of the United Kingdom and Head of the Commonwealth, has travelled more than any other monarch. She has visited each Commonwealth country at least once – often more – and has received Commonwealth and world leaders in her own country.

Even before she became Queen she undertook formal visits on behalf of her ailing father to Canada and the United States in 1951, and to Africa the following year, where she learnt that she had become Queen on his death.

She became the first British monarch to visit Australia and New Zealand when she and the Duke of Edinburgh toured the Antipodes in 1954. During that decade they made 23 State and Commonwealth visits to countries as diverse as Nigeria and the United States, France and Portugal and the Cocos Islands. The commissioning of HMS *Britannia* early in 1954 saw this new Royal Yacht carry the royal couple on a state visit to Libya that year. The young Prince Charles and Princess Anne were able to join their parents on a return leg of the voyage.

In 1992 The Queen had her first meeting with the newly elected President of South Africa, Nelson Mandela, when she was attending the Commonwealth Heads of Government Conference in Zimbabwe. A friendship developed between the two leaders which was apparent in 1996 when the President came to England, joining The Queen in a carriage drive through London and referring to

her as 'My friend Elizabeth'. They met again in 2008 at Buckingham Palace when Mandela was celebrating his 90th birthday.

Canada was the first Commonwealth country visited by The Queen who has since spent 222 days there – including a nine-day visit in 2010 when Michael Ignatieff, the then leader of the country's Liberal Party, said she was 'an absolute joy to meet'.

The Queen has travelled by elephant in Jaipur and been transported by a decorated boat carried aloft by the bare-chested men of Tuvalu. She has ridden in carriages and phaetons galore and enjoyed a water-ride in Copenhagen's Tivoli Gardens. During visits to countries where her usual costume would not be appropriate, she has donned locally acceptable dress – for example, a full-length blue silk outfit in Saudi Arabia and traditional black when she met the Pope at the Vatican in 1980. At other times she finds herself wearing gifts – such as a ceremonial Maori cloak during a tour of New Zealand.

Recent state visits overseas have included a six-day trip to the United Arab Emirates and Oman in November 2010 to cement relationships with the Crown Prince of Abu Dhabi, General Sheikh Mohammed bin Zayed bin Sultan Al Nahyan and His Majesty Sultan Qaboos bin Said of Oman, who was celebrating his 40th year as ruler.

Before being decommissioned in 1997, the Royal Yacht *Britannia* carried members of the Royal Family and dignitaries on 696 foreign visits. She is now at moorings in Leith, Edinburgh, as a popular visitor attraction.

Left: The Royal Yacht *Britannia*, bearing The Queen, the Duke of Edinburgh, Prince Charles and Princess Anne, returning from their 1954 Commonwealth Tour, moves slowly through London's Tower Bridge.

Top right: An unusual mode of transport was enjoyed by The Queen in Banaras during the royal tour to India in January 1961.

Centre right: Two world leaders: Her Majesty The Queen and Nelson Mandela, in October 1992.

Right: The Queen attends a garden party at Government House in Ottawa, Canada, during her tour of the country in June 2010.

Closer to home, The Queen and Prince Philip paid an historically important, and sometimes emotional, visit to Ireland in May 2011. The Queen, delighting her hosts by wearing Irish green, joined President Mary McAleese in laying a wreath in Dublin's Garden of Remembrance. The following day, at the state dinner in Dublin Castle, she made specific reference to the troubled past.

'The relationship has not always been straightforward; nor has the record over the centuries been entirely benign,' she said. 'It is a sad and regrettable reality that through history our islands have experienced more than their fair share of heartache, turbulence and loss.

'With the benefit of historical hindsight we can all see things which we would wish had been done differently or not at all.'

The Queen is Head of the Commonwealth, a voluntary association of 53 independent countries, existing to foster international cooperation and trade links between people the world over.

Below: The Queen shares a joke with fishmonger Pat O'Connell at the English Market, Cork, during her historic four-day visit to the Republic of Ireland in May 2011.

Left: The late American president Ronald Reagan
shared The Queen's love of horse riding. Here
they ride out at Windsor Castle in 1982.

Entertaining at Home

The Queen goes out of her way to prepare herself for any visit she makes, in order to understand the culture of the country and the personal likes and dislikes of her hosts. The same is true when she receives visitors at Buckingham Palace, Windsor or – less often – at Balmoral or Sandringham. She is the perfect hostess, concerned that visitors should be comfortable and at ease.

Visiting heads of state stay in the three-roomed Belgian Suite at Buckingham Palace. During their visit they will be guests of honour at a state banquet to which around 170 guests are invited. Nothing is left to chance. Menus and seating arrangements are planned months in advance so that the evening runs smoothly. The programme for the visit is also organized down to the last detail.

In May 2011, when President Barack Obama and the First Lady, his wife, Michelle, were invited to Buckingham Palace, they received a welcome on the West Terrace with the Scots Guards forming a Guard of Honour, the band playing the American National Anthem, and a march past taking place. After an inspection of the Guard by the President and the Duke of Edinburgh, two Royal Salutes of 41 guns and 62 guns were fired in Green Park and at the Tower of London respectively. At that evening's state banquet Her Majesty told her guests, 'We are here to celebrate the tried, tested and – yes – special relationship between our two countries.'

Right: American president
Barack Obama enjoying a
State Visit to Britain at the
invitation of The Queen
in May 2011.

THE QUEEN'S *Style*

With a busy round of engagements involving up to five changes of outfit in any one day, each of The Queen's ensembles has to be carefully chosen to meet the needs of the occasion. Her entire wardrobe, numbered and catalogued, is stored in huge cupboards on the second floor of Buckingham Palace, where her three dressers can access exactly what is needed. They are the ones who choose what she shall wear each day, although she will have taken the decision on the colour, material and style of each outfit when it was made for her.

Above: An appropriately named Queen Elizabeth rose is planted by Her Majesty at the Royal Foundation of St Katharine in London in March 2011.

Left: The Queen, in a striking peach-coloured outfit, attends the Commonwealth Observance Service at Westminster Abbey in March 2011.

Her Majesty's Hats

Her Majesty is rarely seen without a hat – and there have been some memorable creations over the years. When she started carrying out royal engagements her mother, the late Queen Elizabeth, gave her a sound piece of advice: never to wear a hat with a brim that shielded her face. Photographers the world over have been grateful for that advice, and a small-brimmed or brimless hat is much easier to handle when stepping in and out of cars and carriages – both hands are free for holding handbags and any support needed, rather than having to hang on to a hat that may be caught by a breeze or knocked out of position.

Above: Dressed in the outfit she probably enjoys wearing more than any other, The Queen is seen here at Windsor Horse Show in May 1988.

The Queen has always considered the clothes she must wear as an ever-changing uniform – part of the job. When she is off-duty she is more comfortable in headscarves, tweeds and wellington boots than the formal hats, coordinating dresses and jackets and court shoes that she must wear on most days.

Above: Happy snappers photograph a smiling Queen wearing a stylish pink hat by Frederick Fox as she takes a walkabout in London during her Silver Jubilee celebrations in 1977.

In the early years of Her Majesty's reign many of her hats were created by Simone Mirman, a talented hatmaker with a list of famous clients and who was head of the hat department of Schiaparelli's London branch before the Second World War. One memorable Mirman hat was the yellow silk Tudor-inspired 'gable hood' worn by The Queen when she invested Prince Charles as Prince of Wales in 1969 (pictured on page 47). Frederick Fox, another of her favourite milliners, was the designer of the much-photographed pink hat, decorated with bells, that she wore to mark her Silver Jubilee in 1977.

In later years her style has changed to crisper, more sculptural creations, such as the Angela Kelly-designed primrose-yellow hat trimmed with handmade silk roses and apricot-coloured leaves that she wore to the wedding of Prince William, her grandson, in April 2011.

When she married in 1947, Princess Elizabeth asked her mother's dress designer, Norman Hartnell, to create her wedding gown. From the three designs he supplied she chose one decorated with thousands of seed pearls.

Hartnell, couturier Hardy Amies and dressmaker Ian Thomas were among the leading designers to make her daytime outfits and evening gowns for many years.

A bright mimosa-yellow silk-chiffon gown, decorated with sequinned sprigs of mimosa (wattle) and matching cape, made in 1974 by Ian Thomas, was never worn on the tour of Australia for which it was intended: unfortunately the visit ended early because of a General Election at home. On her Commonwealth tour of Australia 20 years previously she had been presented with a stunning diamond brooch resembling a spray of mimosa and has taken care to wear this brooch on subsequent trips to Australia.

More recent outfits have been made by Maureen Rose, who worked with Ian Thomas for many years until his death in 1993, and who has continued to design clothes for The Queen. It was Maureen Rose who was asked to make the two black dresses The Queen wore when she visited Pope John Paul II at the Vatican – firstly in 1980

Above: Dresses by designers Sir Norman Hartnell, Sir Hardy Amies and Ian Thomas seen here on display at Buckingham Palace in July 2006.

When The Queen is visiting another country her dresser has to take into account not only the climate but also the cultural traditions of the host nation. The colours, fabric and designs are often selected to complement the country's flags or emblems. They are also chosen, at The Queen's insistence, so that she may always clearly be seen in a large crowd.

Below: Designer Angela Kelly made this stunning primrose-yellow single crêpe wool dress with hand-sewn beading at the neck, worn beneath a matching tailored coat, for the wedding in April 2011 of The Queen's grandson, Prince William, to Catherine Middleton.

Above: Her trademark pearls adorning her neck, The Queen arrives at the Vatican in 2000 in a black outfit by Maureen Rose and veiled hat by Frederick Fox.

and again in 2000. Another of her outfits for that trip won high acclaim when the Italian press called Her Majesty 'The Queen of Fashion'. The gown they fell in love with was made of heavy ice-blue crêpe, embroidered with aquamarine thread and trimmed with silver lace, made for a state banquet.

The Queen normally wears plain colours during the day, often in pastel, although her 60th birthday in 1983 was marked with a striking deep yellow outfit, while emerald green was chosen for her first visit to Iceland seven years later. Her evening gowns, of silk, chiffon or crêpe, are sometimes decorated with hand-sewn pearls, crystals, beads and sequins.

She often wears pearls during the day, chosen from her huge collection of jewellery. The dazzling Diamond Diadem that she is pictured wearing on coins and stamps is set with 1,333 diamonds. It was made in 1821 and is always worn when she travels to the State Opening of Parliament.

Portraits OF THE QUEEN

Queen Elizabeth II is the most-photographed woman in the world – and has sat for more than 130 official portraits. They range from Lucien Freud's controversial 2001 painting to Isobel Peachy's 2010 image of her wearing a becoming blue dress and the diamond necklace and earrings made for Queen Victoria, her great-great-grandmother, that she wore at her coronation.

A surprise painting was one by singer and artist Rolf Harris in 2005, showing her wearing green and looking rather jolly, in contrast to the more formal portrait the following year by Jemma Phipps, commissioned by the Ascot Authority to celebrate Her Majesty's 80th birthday and the redevelopment of the racecourse. The Queen, dressed in pale pink, is holding a white handbag, gloves and a race programme.

Possibly the most famous image of all is Pietro Annigoni's 1954 portrait of her wearing the robes of the Order of the Garter.

Pietro Annigoni's famous 1954 portrait was painted over 15 sittings, but the artist struggled to achieve the effect he wanted. The Queen, sensing his difficulties, started chatting to him in French, telling him her childhood game of sitting at windows and imagining the lives of people she saw below. This helped Annigoni to relax and he was able to combine a feeling of regal grandeur and dignity with the sense of a very human woman playing her role to perfection yet still able to look outwards.

Left: The iconic portrait of The Queen by Pietro Annigoni.

An exhibition of almost a hundred photographs of The Queen taken by Cecil Beaton, some previously unseen, will be on show during February to April 2012 at the Victoria and Albert Museum in London. They will range from formal photographs of the Princess Elizabeth to some tender images of The Queen holding her own young children.

Below: A relaxed Queen Elizabeth on board the Royal Yacht *Britannia* in March 1971, captured on film by Patrick Lichfield.

Many of these pictures will be on show during Jubilee year in a National Portrait Gallery touring exhibition which opened in June 2011 in Edinburgh. They include an image of a happy and relaxed Queen, tanned and wearing sunglasses and a sundress, caught in an unguarded moment by photographer Patrick Lichfield in 1971, roaring with laughter at the rail of the Royal Yacht *Britannia*.

Another iconic image is that by American celebrity photographer Annie Leibovitz who captured The Queen in 2007 sitting thoughtfully in the White Drawing Room at Buckingham Palace, the light from the opened French window highlighting the subtle colouring of her pale gold evening dress. She wears a fur stole and a diamond tiara.

But perhaps one of the most imaginative and striking images ever made was commissioned in 2004 by the Island of Jersey from artist Chris Levine, who came up with a royal blue hologram of Her Majesty, entitled *Equanimity and Lightness of Being*.

ACKNOWLEDGEMENTS·

All photographs by kind permission of Getty Images except for:
Alamy: 34 (Corbis Bridge), 36cr (Colin Palmer Photography), 38 (Gerry Walden);
Camera Press: fc; Heather Hook: 35; Mary Evans Picture Library: 59cr and 62
(Illustrated London News).

Quotations are reproduced by kind permission of: p21 Curtis Brown Ltd, London,
on behalf of The Estate of Winston Churchill © Winston S. Churchill;
p30 Daily Mirror © Mirrorpix.

SELECT BIBLIOGRAPHY

Her Majesty, Fifty Regal Years (Brian Hoey, HarperCollins, 2001)
Life With The Queen (Brian Hoey, Sutton Publishing, 2006)
Queen Elizabeth, A Biography (Judith Campbell, Artus Books Ltd, 1979)